LIVE WELL, LEAD WELL

Managing Your Wellbeing and Mental Wellness in Leadership

EVA M. FRANCIS

Copyright © 2024 Eva M. Francis
ALL RIGHTS RESERVED

The content of this book is the intellectual property of Eva M. Francis; therefore, no part of this book may be reproduced, duplicated, or transmitted in either electronic means or printed format in any form without the author's written permission, except for short quotations used for publishing articles or reviews.

First Printing: 2024

ISBN: 9798305184310

Email: info@brillianthealthcaregroup.com

Published by Brilliant Healthcare Publishing

DISCLAIMER

The information provided in this book is intended for educational and informational purposes only. It is designed to support and inspire leaders in their personal and professional wellness journeys. However, it should not be used as a substitute for professional medical advice, diagnosis, or treatment.

While I strive to present accurate and up-to-date information, the field of wellness is constantly evolving. The strategies and practices discussed in this book may not be suitable for everyone, and individual results may vary. Readers are encouraged to consult with qualified healthcare providers, mental health professionals, or wellness coaches before making any significant changes to their lifestyle, diet, or health practices.

The author and publisher of this book disclaim any liability or responsibility for any adverse effects or consequences arising from the use or application of the information contained herein. The reader assumes full responsibility for their own health and wellness decisions.

Additionally, the experiences and insights shared in this book are based on personal anecdotes, research, and the author's observations. They do not guarantee outcomes and should not be interpreted as a promise of specific results. Each leader's journey is unique, and it is essential to find what works best for you.

By reading this book, you acknowledge that you have read and understood this disclaimer, and you agree to hold the author and publisher harmless from any claims arising from your use of the information provided.

DEDICATION

To all leaders who embody integrity, kindness, and authenticity, I dedicate this book to you, for your unwavering commitment to leading with heart and purpose.

Most profoundly, I honor my beloved parents, Mr. Vincent Francis and Mrs. Eunice Francis. You were my first teachers in the art of leadership, instilling in me values that would guide my journey through life.

From an early age, you recognized my potential and entrusted me with responsibilities, allowing me to step into the role of a leader as the first among my siblings to embark on the path of high school.

Your faith in me was a gift that shaped my identity and instilled a sense of responsibility that I carry to this day. You taught me that true leadership is not merely about authority, but about serving others, fostering connections, and lifting those around you. Your kindness and integrity were the cornerstones of your lives, and it is through your example that I learned the importance of leading with compassion and authenticity.

As I pen these words, I reflect on the countless lessons you imparted, the sacrifices you made, and the love you shared, which continue to inspire me to lead with the same spirit you exemplified.

This book is a tribute to you and to all those who strive to make a difference in the world, guided by the principles of kindness and integrity. Thank you for believing in me and for laying the foundation of my journey.

CONTENTS

Disclaimer	3
Dedication	5
What to Expect	9
Preface	11
Chapter 1	*15*
Introduction to Wellness and Wellbeing in Leadership	15
Chapter 2	*18*
The Foundations of Holistic Health	18
Chapter 3	*22*
The Leader's Guide to Physical Wellness	22
Chapter 4	*26*
Brain Health and Leadership	26
Chapter 5	*31*
Cultivating Mental Resilience	31
Chapter 6	*37*
Enhancing Emotional Intelligence	37
Chapter 7	*41*
Spiritual Well-being and Purpose-Driven Leadership	41
Chapter 8	*48*
Building Stronger Relationships	48
Chapter 9	*54*
Creating a Culture of Wellness at Work	54
Chapter 10	*59*
Time Management and Work-Life Balance	59

Chapter 11 — 64
   Sustaining Wellness for Long Term Leadership Success — 64
Chapter 12 — 67
   Essential Lifestyle Changes for Optimal Well-Being — 67
Conclusion — 70
About the Author — 72

WHAT TO EXPECT

In "Live Well, Lead Well," you will embark on a transformative journey that intertwines the principles of effective leadership with the essential practices of health and wellness. This book is designed for leaders at all levels who recognize that their personal well-being directly impacts their ability to lead others.

You will experience:

1. *A Holistic Approach to Leadership:* You will discover how physical, mental, and emotional health are interconnected and vital to successful leadership. The book provides a framework for integrating wellness practices into your everyday leadership routines.

2. *Practical Strategies:* Each chapter offers actionable tips and techniques that you can easily implement. From how to relax to nutrition guidelines, you will learn how to prioritize your health without sacrificing your professional responsibilities.

3. *Personal Stories and Case Studies:* This book includes inspiring anecdotes and real-world examples from some of my stories as a leader and many others who have successfully embraced wellness in their lives. It also includes organizations demonstrating the positive impact of wellness on productivity, team morale, and overall workplace culture.

4. *Self-Reflection Exercises:* You will engage in thought-provoking exercises designed to encourage self-awareness and personal growth. These exercises would prompt you to assess your current well-being and identify areas for improvement.

5. *Building a Wellness Culture:* This book emphasizes the importance of fostering a culture of wellness within organizations. You will learn how to model healthy behaviors, create supportive environments, and inspire your team to prioritize their own health.

6. *Sustainable Practices:* You will gain insights into developing sustainable wellness habits that can be maintained over the long term. The focus is on creating a balanced lifestyle that enhances both personal and professional effectiveness.

By the end of "Live Well, Lead Well," you will feel empowered to take charge of your health and well-being, ultimately becoming a more effective, compassionate, and resilient leader.

PREFACE

When I transitioned from Jamaica to the USA as a nurse, I faced a profound culture shock. The unfamiliarity of the new environment was daunting, but I was determined to succeed. As the first child in my family to attend college, I carried the weight of my family's hopes and dreams on my shoulders. My goal was clear: to uplift and support my loved ones.

I eagerly awaited the day I could work in the Intensive Care Unit (ICU). To me, becoming an ICU nurse represented a significant achievement—a testament to my hard work and dedication. When that day finally arrived, I felt a rush of excitement and anticipation. However, just one week into my new role, everything changed. The director informed me that I was not "ICU material" and dismissed me from the position.

I was devastated. The tears flowed as I grappled with feelings of embarrassment and shame. Returning to my previous department felt like a demotion, especially after they had celebrated my transition with a send-off party. It was a humbling experience, and I struggled with feelings of worthlessness.

Yet, despite the humiliation, my colleagues welcomed me back with open arms. Their support reminded me that I was not alone in this journey. I made the resolute decision to work even harder.

One year later, I found another opportunity at a different hospital, where I performed exceptionally well. Over the years, I was promoted several times—each promotion a recognition of my potential, even when I struggled to see it in myself. My supervisors believed in me, often seeing qualities in me that I had yet to recognize.

Throughout my career, I have held various leadership positions across multiple specialty areas, including Critical Care, the Emergency Department, Dialysis, Orthopedics, and more. Many of my promotions resulted from my contributions being recognized by others; often, I learned that my name was mentioned in discussions when I was not present. I have never actively sought promotions; instead, my leaders identified my potential and entrusted me with the responsibility of revitalizing departments that were struggling to grow. In addition to my leadership roles, I have had the privilege of mentoring and coaching hundreds of nurses and nurse leaders as they transitioned into leadership and specialty roles. I am honored to have received several leadership awards, including the Healthcare Leadership Awards for South Florida, a Community Humanitarian Award, and a Leadership Award in the category of Mentorship and Coaching. Throughout my journey, I have been fortunate to have mentors who believed in me, encouraged me, and provided invaluable support at every step.

After several years in various hospital roles, I found myself increasingly drawn to entrepreneurship. While the predictable salary and stable routine of a hospital job were comforting, a growing part of me craved the excitement and unpredictability of starting my own venture. With a mix of excitement and trepidation, I made the bold decision to leave the hospital and embrace the challenges of entrepreneurship.

The first few years were undeniably tough. I failed many times, largely due to my lack of business knowledge. I had no coaching or mentoring, and I did not always use my time wisely. However, these initial failures were critical, teaching me the essential skills needed to build and sustain a successful business.

Recognizing my shortcomings, I knew a strategic shift was necessary. I transitioned my consulting firm into a healthcare staffing business, a move that perfectly aligned with my background and the growing demand for quality healthcare professionals. This change, along with my relentless determination to succeed, began to yield results.

Despite many challenges along the way, I built Brilliant Healthcare Staffing—a high-income business that stands as a testament to perseverance, resilience, and the power of a dream. Every day, we work to connect exceptional healthcare professionals with opportunities where they can make a significant impact, just as I once did at the bedside.

What's my message? If I can do it, so can you. The healthcare staffing industry urgently needs great talent. It is an industry that not only offers immense opportunities for growth and success but also enables you to make a meaningful difference in the lives of others.

Not only the healthcare industry, but every industry is in a critical state that needs the attention of well-rounded leaders. This book will serve as a road map for you to become such a leader.

Chapter 1

Introduction to Wellness and Wellbeing in Leadership

Leadership is beyond making decisions and overseeing operations. While everyone is often concerned about a leader's actions and how they affect the organization, the leader's wellness is often overlooked, but it is a crucial aspect of effective leadership. A leader is only as effective as their health.

What is Wellness in Leadership?

Wellness in leadership extends beyond physical health to encompass mental and emotional well-being. It involves striking a balance between personal and professional life, managing stress effectively, and cultivating a positive mindset. A leader who prioritizes their wellness is better positioned to inspire and guide others toward success.

Why is Wellness in Leadership Important?

Without placing health and wellness at the forefront, it becomes nearly impossible to lead effectively. Here's why:

- ❖ *Enhanced Decision-Making:* Leaders who maintain their physical and mental well-being are better equipped to make sound decisions under pressure and navigate challenges with clarity.

- ❖ *Increased Productivity:* Wellness in leadership promotes higher levels of energy, focus, and motivation, resulting in greater productivity and improved overall performance.

- ❖ *Positive Organizational Culture:* Leaders who prioritize their wellness set a powerful example for their teams, fostering a culture of health and well-being within the organization.

- ❖ *Employee Engagement and Retention:* Employees are more engaged and loyal to leaders who value wellness, which enhances job satisfaction and boosts retention.

- ❖ *Long-Term Success*: True leadership success is more than short-term achievements; it is about sustaining well-being over time. Leaders who prioritize their wellness are better equipped for long-term success and fulfillment.

Self-Care as a Leadership Strategy

Self-care is not just vital for personal well-being; it is also a powerful business and leadership strategy. When we take care of ourselves, we show up as our best selves at work, making better decisions, increasing productivity, and fostering positive relationships with colleagues and clients.

By prioritizing self-care, we become better equipped to handle stress and avoid burnout, ultimately leading to greater job satisfaction and success. Whether through taking regular breaks, practicing relaxation, or setting boundaries, self-care is essential to maintaining a healthy work-life balance.

So, next time you are feeling overwhelmed or burnt out at work, remember that taking care of yourself is not only beneficial for your personal well-being, but it can also be a smart business move. Prioritize self-care and watch how it positively impacts your professional life.

Wellness in leadership is not a luxury but a necessity for creating a thriving and successful organization. By prioritizing your well-being, you will inspire, motivate, and lead your team towards a brighter and healthier future. In the journey of leadership, remember that taking care of yourself is not selfish; it is essential for leading others effectively and making a lasting impact.

Chapter 2

The Foundations of Holistic Health

I vividly remember a time when I felt mentally drained as a leader, with my team expecting more from me than I felt capable of giving. The pressure to perform, make difficult decisions, and constantly operate at my best took a serious toll on my mental well-being. I struggled to focus and felt overwhelmed by the responsibilities on my shoulders.

Realizing I could not lead effectively in that state, I made the difficult choice to step back and prioritize my holistic health. I took time off to recharge, practiced relaxation, and sought support from a therapist. As I focused on my mental and emotional well-being, I gradually regained clarity, resilience, and a renewed sense of purpose.

Through this challenging experience, I learned how critical it is for leaders to prioritize their holistic health. By taking care of myself, I was able to show up for my team in a more present, empathetic, and effective way. This period of self-reflection and self-care not only improved my personal well-being but also had a positive ripple effect on my team and the overall organizational culture.

Stepping back and prioritizing my holistic health became a turning point in my leadership journey. It taught me that true strength as a leader doesn't come from pushing through burnout and exhaustion but from taking the time to nurture and replenish all aspects of my well-being. In doing so, I became a more balanced, resilient, and inspiring leader.

As a leader, it is essential to understand that true success is not solely about achieving workplace goals; it is about cultivating holistic health across all areas of life. Holistic health extends beyond physical fitness to include mental, emotional, and spiritual well-being.

Physical Health

The physical aspect of holistic health is often the most visible and tangible. Regular exercise, proper nutrition, and sufficient rest are fundamental components of physical well-being. As a leader, taking care of your body sets a positive example for your team and gives you the energy and stamina to face challenges head-on.

Mental Health

Mental health is just as important as physical health, particularly in high-pressure leadership roles. Practicing relaxation, employing stress management techniques, and seeking support when necessary are vital to maintaining mental well-being. A clear and focused mind is key to making sound decisions and leading with confidence.

Emotional Health

Emotional health involves understanding and managing your emotions effectively. As a leader, it is essential to be in tune with your own feelings as well as those of your team members. Cultivating emotional intelligence, practicing empathy, and fostering positive relationships help create a supportive and harmonious work environment. Leaders who prioritize emotional health can better manage their own emotions, understand those of others, and maintain strong, positive relationships with their teams.

Spiritual Health

Spiritual health involves finding meaning, purpose, and connection in your life. This can be achieved through religious practices, meditation, or simply spending time in nature. Nurturing your spiritual well-being fosters a sense of inner peace, resilience, and a broader perspective on both leadership and life.

Occupational Health

Occupational health in leadership means striking a balance between work responsibilities and personal well-being. Leaders who prioritize occupational health set boundaries, delegate tasks, and practice effective time management to prevent burnout. As well as, maintaining a sustainable workload.

Financial Health

Financial health is often overlooked as a crucial aspect of leadership, yet it significantly impacts overall well-being. Leaders who are financially healthy make sound financial decisions, manage resources effectively, and prioritize long-term financial stability for themselves and their organizations. By taking control of your finances, you can reduce stress, boost confidence, and focus on your leadership responsibilities with clarity and purpose.

Integration

Holistic health is not about compartmentalizing different aspects of your well-being; it is about integrating them into a cohesive whole. Your physical, mental, emotional, and spiritual health are all interconnected and none should be prioritized over the other. To achieve a balanced and fulfilling life as a leader, you need to integrate all.

You must recognize that success is not solely defined by professional achievements but also by the well-being of your mind, body, and spirit.

Moreover, as a leader, your actions speak louder than words. By prioritizing your holistic health, you demonstrate to your team the importance of self-care, work-life balance, and overall well-being. Leading by example inspires others to adopt similar practices, creating a culture of health and wellness within your organization. Thereby leading to greater efficiency of your organization and the attainment of your goals.

Chapter 3

The Leader's Guide to Physical Wellness

Leadership is a demanding journey, and whether you are stepping into it for the first time or have years of experience, one truth remains undeniable: your success as a leader is closely tied to adopting a "wellness" mindset. Healthy leaders are winning leaders.

Wellness, in this context, goes beyond physical health. It begins with you—a healthy mindset that radiates outward, shaping your ability to inspire your team, achieve goals, and drive meaningful change within your organization. Yet, despite its significance, this essential aspect of leadership is often overlooked.

Too many organizations today are marked by unhealthy leaders—those whose limited mindsets, insecurities, and disregard for personal and team wellness create environments where employees struggle to thrive. Perhaps you've witnessed this firsthand or even struggled with it yourself. The good news is, you can change that narrative.

In this post-pandemic era, the urgency to prioritize wellness in the workplace has never been greater. As a leader, your role in fostering this transformation is pivotal. The journey begins with you. When you prioritize self-care and wellness, you don't just lead effectively—you inspire others to do the same. And at the core of this transformation is your physical wellness, which empowers you to lead with clarity, resilience, and energy.

Exercise Routines for Leaders

Regular exercise is essential for maintaining your physical health and enhancing your leadership capabilities. You may feel that fitting physical activity into your already packed schedule is daunting, but it Is not only achievable; it is vital. Simple activities like a quick morning workout, a brisk walk during lunch, or a strength training session after work can make all the difference.

The key is to find an exercise routine that works for you and stick with it. When you prioritize physical activity, you improve not only your health but also your ability to handle the demands of leadership. Regular exercise enhances your stamina, sharpens your focus, and boosts your confidence—all of which are essential for navigating the complexities of leadership.

Nutritional Guidelines

What you eat directly impacts how you lead. As a leader, fueling your body with nourishing foods is critical to maintaining your energy levels and overall performance. A balanced diet that includes fruits, vegetables, lean proteins, and whole grains provides the nutrients you need to stay sharp and effective.

You do not have to overhaul your diet overnight, but small, intentional changes can yield significant benefits. Start by incorporating more whole, unprocessed foods into your meals and staying hydrated throughout the day. Mindful eating not only supports your physical health but also helps you maintain the energy and focus needed to lead with excellence.

Sleep Hygiene Tips

Quality sleep is non-negotiable for you as a leader. It is the foundation of your cognitive function, emotional resilience, and physical health. Yet, it is often the first thing sacrificed in the face of deadlines and responsibilities.

To prioritize quality sleep, create a bedtime routine that helps you wind down. Establish a consistent sleep schedule, make your sleeping environment comfortable, and minimize screen time before bed. When you commit to better sleep hygiene, you will wake up refreshed and equipped to tackle the challenges of leadership with clarity and focus. Your physical wellness is not just about your health; it is a cornerstone of your leadership success. By prioritizing regular exercise, nourishing nutrition, and restorative sleep, you equip yourself to lead with resilience, energy, and focus. These practices aren't just good for you—they set a powerful example for your team, inspiring them to pursue their own well-being.

As you strive to make a meaningful impact in your organization and beyond, remember that caring for yourself is not a distraction from your role as a leader; it is an essential part of fulfilling it.

Chapter 4

Brain Health and Leadership

Leadership is not merely a position, title, or personality trait; it is a brain function. Every decision a leader makes, every conflict they resolve, every vision they cast, and every relationship they nurture begins in the brain. The brain is the command center of leadership. Yet, for decades, we have trained leaders in strategy, communication, and organizational skills without ever addressing the organ that drives it all. To lead well, we must first think well. And to think well, the brain must be healthy.

Why Brain Health Matters in Leadership

The brain is responsible for processing information, regulating emotions, interpreting experiences, and determining your response to challenges. Leaders who do not understand their own brain are often reactive instead of responsive, stressed instead of strategic, and burnt out instead of purposeful.

A compromised brain produces compromised leadership. A stressed brain struggles to innovate. An anxious brain avoids risk and opportunity. An exhausted brain misreads people and intentions. A distracted brain cannot lead with clarity. A fearful brain cannot make courageous decisions

If leadership begins in the brain, then ignoring brain health is not just unwise; it is irresponsible.

The Neuroscience Behind Leadership

The brain contains three primary areas that significantly influence leadership:

1. The Prefrontal Cortex: The CEO of the Brain

This region governs decision-making, vision casting, emotional regulation, problem-solving, and goal orientation. When the prefrontal cortex is optimized, leaders think with clarity, communicate with wisdom, and act with purpose. When it is overwhelmed or fatigued, leaders become impulsive, indecisive, and emotionally scattered.

2. The Amygdala: The Fear and Survival Center

This area detects threats. When overactivated, leaders misinterpret feedback as a personal attack, lead defensively, avoid innovation, and resist necessary change. A leader whose amygdala is in constant alarm cannot build trust, collaborate, or inspire.

3. The Hippocampus: The Memory and Learning Center

Healthy leaders must learn continuously. A neglected brain sabotages retention, creativity, and adaptability, which are three qualities essential for modern leadership.

As a leader, you cannot afford to neglect your brain's health. When you do so, you carry emotional baggage into decisions, react instead of responding, improve systems while you ignore yourself, and inspire others while you are drowning. Your leadership capacity rises or falls to the level of your brain's health.

Neuroplasticity: The Leader's Advantage

The most powerful discovery in modern brain science is neuroplasticity. Neuroplasticity is the brain's ability to rewire itself through intentional thought and repeated action. This means that you are not stuck with the brain you have. You can literally build the brain you need to lead at a higher level.

Strategies for Brain-Based Leadership

To strengthen the brain and enhance leadership ability, leaders must invest in:

1. **Rest**

Sleep is not optional. It is neurological maintenance. Leaders who brag about lack of sleep are unknowingly shrinking their hippocampus.

2. **Exercise**

Physical movement releases BDNF (Brain-Derived Neurotrophic Factor), which acts like fertilizer for brain cells, improving memory, focus, and mood.

3. **Nutrition**

The brain is 60% fat. What you eat either fuels brain function or fogs it.

4. **Thought Management**

Your thoughts sculpt your brain. Negative thinking wires the brain for fear; intentional thinking wires it for faith, clarity, and innovation.

5. **Purpose**

A brain without direction becomes anxious. Purpose stabilizes neural patterns and creates emotional resilience.

The Future of Leadership Is Neurological

We are stepping into a new era where leadership training will not be complete without brain education. The leader of the future must understand:

- How the brain reacts under stress
- How to build neural pathways for success
- How emotional intelligence emerges from brain function
- How identity is shaped by thought patterns
- How brain health determines influence

Leadership is not only emotional and spiritual; it is neurological. To live well and lead well, the brain must be well. Your brain is your leadership headquarters. When you nurture it, protect it, and intentionally shape it, you unlock a level of clarity, confidence, creativity, and conviction that cannot be taught in a classroom. You do not lead from your title; you lead from your brain.

Healthy brains create healthy leaders, and healthy leaders change the world.

Chapter 5

Cultivating Mental Resilience

When Nelson Mandela emerged from 27 years of imprisonment, he did not seek vengeance; instead, he worked tirelessly to unite a fractured nation. His resilience became a global symbol of triumph over adversity. "Do not judge me by my successes," Mandela once said, "judge me by how many times I fell down and got back up again." This ability to persevere, adapt, and thrive in the face of challenges captures what it means to cultivate mental resilience as a leader.

Leadership demands more than technical skills or intellectual acumen. It requires the mental fortitude to weather challenges, adapt to change, and lead with confidence under pressure. As a leader, your ability to stay composed, maintain focus, and inspire your team during tough times is what sets you apart.

Mental resilience is not innate; it Is cultivated. It Is the capacity to recover from setbacks, manage stress, and navigate uncertainty without losing sight of your vision. When you build resilience, you not only enhance your leadership, but also empower your team to follow suit.

Strategies for Cultivating Mental Resilience

Practice Relaxation

Relaxation techniques are invaluable for managing stress and maintaining mental clarity. As Franklin D. Roosevelt once said, "Calm seas never made a skilled sailor." You cannot become a successful leader until you've navigated tough and turbulent seasons.

Positive meditation and deep breathing exercises can help you stay centered in high-pressure situations. Lately, there has been an emphasis on breathwork. Breathwork is a practice that uses breathing techniques to improve mental, physical, and emotional health. Breathwork can be beneficial to your wellness; however, please consult your physician before beginning any breathwork therapy. These techniques reduce anxiety and enhance self-awareness, enabling you to make thoughtful decisions.

Build a Support Network

Even the most resilient leaders understand the value of community. "Alone we can do so little; together we can do so much." Helen Keller famously said. Surrounding yourself with trusted colleagues, mentors, and friends provides a critical safety net during difficult times.

For instance, during the Cuban Missile Crisis, John F. Kennedy leaned on a close circle of advisors to weigh decisions that could have led to nuclear war. Their counsel and support helped him navigate one of the most perilous moments in history with composure and resolve. By cultivating meaningful connections, you gain access to diverse perspectives, emotional support, and practical advice—all of which strengthen your resilience.

Embrace Failure as a Learning Opportunity
Failure is a universal experience, but resilient leaders see it as a stepping stone to growth. As Theodore Roosevelt once remarked, "The only man who never makes mistakes is the man who never does anything."

Instead of fearing failure, approach it with curiosity. Reflect on what went wrong, identify lessons learned, and apply those insights to future endeavors. As I am writing this, the story of Oprah Winfrey came to mind. She was fired from her first television job and told she was "unfit for TV." Rather than giving up, she used the experience to fuel her passion and later became one of the most influential media figures in history.

Cultivate Purpose
Resilience thrives on purpose. When you have a clear sense of why you lead, it becomes easier to endure hardships. Viktor Frankl, a

Holocaust survivor, encapsulated this in his book *Man's Search for Meaning*, "Those who have a 'why' to live can bear almost any 'how.' "

Purpose-driven leaders inspire their teams by focusing on a shared vision. During the COVID-19 pandemic, New Zealand Prime Minister Jacinda Ardern exemplified this by consistently communicating her nation's collective purpose: to protect lives and ensure a safe future. Her clarity and empathy galvanized citizens, demonstrating how purpose fortifies resilience.

Develop Adaptability

In this ever-changing world, the ability to adapt is essential for resilience. As Charles Darwin noted, "It is not the strongest of the species that survive, nor the most intelligent, but the one most responsive to change."

Adaptable leaders approach uncertainty with curiosity and openness. They pivot strategies when necessary and encourage their teams to do the same. For example, when the global economy faced a downturn in 2008, Howard Schultz, former CEO of Starbucks, shifted focus from expansion to improving operational efficiency. This adaptability helped the company recover and emerge stronger.

Foster Emotional Agility

Emotional agility—the ability to manage your emotions without being overwhelmed by them—is another cornerstone of resilience. Resilient leaders don't suppress their feelings; they acknowledge and process them constructively. As Michelle Obama wrote in her memoir, *Becoming*, "You can't make decisions based on fear and the possibility of what might happen."

By practicing self-reflection and emotional regulation, you can maintain balance in emotionally charged situations. This helps you respond to challenges thoughtfully rather than react impulsively.

Commit to Lifelong Learning

Resilient leaders are perpetual learners. They embrace change as an opportunity to acquire new skills and insights. Mahatma Gandhi advised, "Live as if you were to die tomorrow. Learn as if you were to live forever."

Lifelong learning expands your perspective, builds confidence, and equips you to handle challenges more effectively. Whether through reading, attending workshops, or seeking mentorship, continuous learning enhances your adaptability and resilience.

Resilience is not about avoiding challenges—it's about facing them with courage, adaptability, and tenacity. As a leader, your ability to cultivate mental resilience will inspire your team, strengthen your organization, and shape your legacy.

Challenges will come, but with resilience, you will not only endure—you will thrive. Let Nelson Mandela's words always motivate you in your down moments: "It is not about how many times you fall, but how many times you rise again."

Chapter 6

Enhancing Emotional Intelligence

Emotional intelligence (EQ) is the ability to understand, embrace, and manage emotions. First coined in 1990 by researchers John Mayer and Peter Salovey, the concept was popularized by psychologist Daniel Goleman of Harvard Business School. Research indicates that 90% of top performers exhibit high emotional intelligence.

In recent years, emotional intelligence has become increasingly recognized as a critical factor in effective leadership. Leaders with high EQ can understand and manage their own emotions. They can also manage the emotions of others, enabling them to build strong relationships, communicate effectively, and navigate complex situations with empathy and resilience.

The Role of Emotional Intelligence in Leadership

Emotional intelligence encompasses a range of skills and competencies that contribute to effective decision-making, communication, and relationship-building. Leaders who possess high emotional intelligence excel in their roles by developing five essential skills:

- *Self-awareness:* This involves recognizing and understanding one's own emotions, strengths, and weaknesses. Leaders adept at self-awareness are better equipped to perceive and manage the feelings of others, ultimately inspiring their teams. Research shows that leaders lacking self-awareness often make poor decisions and struggle to manage conflict effectively.

- *Self-regulation:* This skill involves managing emotions, behaviors, and impulses while remaining composed under pressure. The more self-aware a leader is, the easier it becomes to self-regulate. Daniel Goleman emphasizes, "In my experience, I have never seen the tendency toward radical outbursts to surface as an indicator of strong leadership." Leaders prone to emotional outbursts can improve their self-regulation through strategies such as pausing before responding, taking a step back, and allowing time to process emotions.

- *Empathy:* Empathy involves understanding and considering the emotions and perspectives of others, making it a top leadership skill in today's challenging business landscape. Research shows that leaders who listen and respond with empathy outperform their peers in coaching, planning, and decision-making by over 40%.

- ❖ *Social skills:* Leaders must build and maintain positive relationships, communicate persuasively, and resolve conflicts constructively.

- ❖ *Motivation:* This refers to the ability to inspire oneself and others to take action. Self-motivated leaders set goals, take initiative, and encourage others while remaining positive and optimistic, especially during turbulent times. A leader's positivity can significantly boost their team's confidence.

Leaders who cultivate these emotional intelligence skills are better equipped to inspire their teams, foster a positive work culture, and drive organizational success.

The Impact of Emotional Intelligence on Leadership Effectiveness

Emotional intelligence plays a crucial role in determining a leader's effectiveness across various domains. Leaders with high EQ can:

Communicate effectively: They convey messages clearly, listen actively, and respond empathetically to team members' needs and concerns.

Make sound decisions: By understanding their own emotions and those of others, emotionally intelligent leaders make well-informed, rational decisions that consider their team's and organization's impact.

Manage conflicts: Leaders with high emotional intelligence navigate conflicts diplomatically, with empathy and a focus on finding mutually beneficial solutions.

Foster collaboration: EQ enables leaders to build trust, inspire loyalty, and create a collaborative environment where team members feel valued and supported.

Emotional intelligence is not just a personal trait but a crucial leadership competency that can significantly impact achieving organizational goals and nurturing a culture of collaboration and growth. It is a vital attribute for effective leadership.

Chapter 7

Spiritual Well-being and Purpose-Driven Leadership

As leaders, recognizing the significance of spiritual well-being is essential for maintaining a healthy and fulfilling life. Spiritual well-being transcends traditional religious definitions; it encompasses a profound sense of connection to something greater than ourselves. This connection can manifest in various forms, such as through nature, community, or the knowledge of God, our Father.

At the core of spiritual well-being lies the belief that our lives have meaning and purpose. Tapping into this sense of purpose equips leaders to navigate the challenges and uncertainties inherent in their roles. When our actions align with our values and beliefs, we can lead with authenticity and integrity. In turn, fostering trust and respect within our teams.

Spiritual well-being is not a static state but a journey of continual growth. It involves cultivating inner peace and harmony through practices that allow us to connect with our inner selves. Activities such as positive affirmation, prayer, bible reading, journaling, or simply spending time in quiet reflection can quiet the mind, offering clarity and perspective on our leadership responsibilities.

"When we are no longer able to change a situation, we are challenged to change ourselves," noted Viktor Frankl, a psychiatrist and Holocaust survivor. Leaders who embrace spiritual practices develop the resilience needed to adapt to life's inevitable challenges and guide their teams with steadiness and grace.

Beyond personal growth, spiritual well-being fosters compassion and empathy—essential traits for effective leadership. Recognizing the interconnectedness of all beings enables leaders to approach others with humility and kindness, qualities that not only strengthen workplace relationships but also contribute to a more inclusive and harmonious organizational culture. This interconnectedness reminds us that our decisions and actions ripple outward, impacting not only our teams but the larger community as well.

Consider, for example, a leader who regularly engages in reflective practices and prioritizes empathy. Such a leader is better equipped to address a team member's concerns with genuine care and understanding, creating an environment where individuals feel valued and supported. This approach, in turn, boosts morale, fosters collaboration, and enhances overall productivity.

≈The Path to Purposeful Leadership

Purposeful leadership is a transformative approach that extends beyond achieving goals or meeting targets. It embodies a deep sense of meaning and intention, guided by values and beliefs aligned with a greater purpose. Purposeful leaders are motivated not just by results but by a desire to make a positive impact on the world and inspire others to do the same.

Self-Reflection: Discovering Your "Why"

The journey toward becoming a purposeful leader begins with self-reflection and introspection. This involves a deliberate examination of our core values, beliefs, and motivations to uncover what truly drives us. Simon Sinek, in his groundbreaking book *Start with Why*, emphasizes, "People don't buy what you do; they buy why you do it." For leaders, understanding their "why" provides the foundation for authentic and impactful leadership.

Self-reflection can take many forms, such as journaling about one's values, seeking feedback from trusted colleagues, or engaging in mindfulness practices. For example, a leader who values community might identify their purpose as fostering a collaborative workplace where everyone feels included and empowered. With this clarity, their decisions and actions naturally align with their overarching purpose, enhancing both their personal fulfillment and their team's success.

Building Deeper Connections

Purposeful leaders prioritize connecting with others on a deeper level. They build strong relationships rooted in trust, empathy, and mutual respect. These connections foster a sense of belonging and community within their teams, creating an environment where individuals feel safe to share ideas, take risks, and grow.

Imagine a leader who takes the time to deeply understand their team members' aspirations and challenges. By offering mentorship, providing resources, and celebrating achievements, the leader not only strengthens their team's capabilities but also cultivates loyalty and commitment. As Brené Brown, a renowned researcher on vulnerability and leadership, asserts, "Connection is why we're here; it is what gives purpose and meaning to our lives."

Embracing Continuous Growth

Purposeful leaders understand that personal and professional development is an ongoing journey. They remain open to new ideas, perspectives, and experiences, actively seeking opportunities for growth. Whether it is attending workshops, reading extensively, or engaging in thoughtful dialogue with peers, these leaders embrace change and innovation as opportunities for improvement.

For example, a leader navigating the challenges of a rapidly evolving industry. By staying informed about emerging trends and encouraging their team to adopt innovative practices, the leader not only enhances their own adaptability but also inspires creativity and resilience within the team. This commitment to learning fosters a culture of growth and adaptability, ensuring long-term success.

Inspiring Through Authenticity and Integrity

Ultimately, purposeful leadership is about leading with authenticity, integrity, and compassion. It involves embodying our values and beliefs in all aspects of our leadership and inspiring others to do the same. Purposeful leaders are not afraid to show vulnerability, admit mistakes, or seek input from their teams. These actions demonstrate humility and create an atmosphere of mutual respect and collaboration.

For instance, during the challenging period of the COVID-19 pandemic, New Zealand's Prime Minister, Jacinda Ardern, exemplified purposeful leadership. She openly communicated the uncertainties and difficulties the nation faced while remaining transparent about the government's plans and decisions. By consistently reinforcing the shared vision of prioritizing public health and community well-being, Ardern fostered trust and unity among citizens. Her authenticity and empathetic approach empowered New Zealanders to collectively navigate the crisis, demonstrating the profound impact of transparency and integrity in leadership.

≈Practical Strategies for Cultivating Purposeful Leadership

1. **Engage in Daily Reflection:** Dedicate time each day to reflect on your actions, decisions, and interactions. Consider how they align with your core values and purpose.
2. **Practice Active Listening:** Show genuine interest in the thoughts and feelings of others. Listening attentively not only builds trust but also deepens your understanding of your team's needs and aspirations.
3. **Set Purpose-Driven Goals:** Align your organizational objectives with your values and vision, ensuring that your goals reflect a greater purpose.
4. **Cultivate Empathy:** Seek to understand the perspectives of others, especially during conflicts or challenging situations. Empathy fosters stronger relationships and more effective problem-solving.
5. **Invest in Personal Growth:** Continuously seek opportunities for learning and development, both for yourself and your team. Encourage a culture of curiosity and innovation.

Spiritual well-being and purposeful leadership are deeply intertwined. Leaders who cultivate their spiritual well-being gain clarity, resilience, and compassion, enabling them to lead with authenticity and integrity. I would love to end this chapter using the words of a great leader, Mahatma Gandhi, he said, "The best way to find yourself is to lose yourself in the service of others."

Chapter 8

Building Stronger Relationships

Success in leadership hinges not only on strategic vision and decision-making but also on the quality of relationships forged along the way. Leadership is not just about wielding authority or driving results; it is deeply rooted in the art of human connection. The relationships you cultivate as a leader shape the culture of your organization, the success of your team, and your personal growth. While qualities like empathy and authenticity are foundational, truly impactful leadership demands going beyond the basics to create connections that inspire trust, loyalty, and collaboration.

The Power of Relational Intelligence

Relational intelligence is the ability to understand, navigate, and manage relationships with intention and skill. It goes beyond emotional intelligence by focusing on the dynamics of interpersonal interactions in a professional setting. As a leader, relational intelligence enables you to assess the needs of your team, adapt your communication style, and foster environments where individuals feel valued and empowered.

For example, some team members thrive on direct feedback, while others may need encouragement to open up during discussions. Relational intelligence equips you to approach each relationship with tailored strategies, ensuring that every individual feels heard and supported.

Trust: The Cornerstone of Leadership Relationships

Trust is the currency of leadership relationships, and it must be earned through consistent actions rather than declarations. Leaders who inspire trust:

1. **Deliver on Promises**: Reliability builds credibility. Follow through on commitments, no matter how small, to demonstrate integrity.
2. **Admit Mistakes**: Vulnerability fosters authenticity. When leaders own up to their errors, they show humility and accountability, which strengthens trust.
3. **Protect Team Interests**: Stand up for your team in challenging situations. Whether it involves advocating for resources or defending them from undue criticism, your actions should reflect a commitment to their well-being.

Trust is a two-way street. While you work to earn the trust of your team, make a conscious effort to trust them in return. Delegate responsibilities, empower decision-making, and resist the urge to micromanage. This mutual trust creates a foundation for innovation, collaboration, and growth.

Embracing Diversity and Inclusion

Strong relationships thrive in environments where diversity is celebrated and inclusion is prioritized. As a leader, it is essential to acknowledge the unique strengths, backgrounds, and perspectives of your team members. Inclusive leadership fosters a sense of belonging, which is critical for building relationships that transcend superficial interactions. How can you achieve this then?

- **Celebrate Differences**: Actively seek out and value diverse viewpoints. Encourage open dialogue where team members feel comfortable expressing their ideas.
- **Address Biases**: Reflect on your own biases and take steps to mitigate them in your interactions and decisions. Promote fairness and equity within your team.
- **Foster Collaboration**: Create opportunities for team members from different backgrounds to work together. Shared goals and collaborative projects can strengthen bonds and deepen mutual respect.

Navigating Conflict with Confidence

Conflict is an inevitable aspect of any relationship, especially in leadership. How you handle disagreements can either strengthen or erode the relationships you've built. Instead of avoiding conflict, embrace it as an opportunity for growth and understanding.

1. **Stay Calm and Objective**: Approach conflicts with a composed mindset. Focus on addressing the issue rather than assigning blame.
2. **Seek to Understand**: Listen to all sides of the story with an open mind. Understanding the underlying concerns can reveal solutions that benefit everyone involved.
3. **Focus on Resolution**: Shift the focus from the problem to the outcome. Collaboratively brainstorm solutions that align with the team's goals and values.

When managed effectively, conflict can strengthen relationships by deepening trust and fostering a culture of accountability and respect.

Building Relationships Beyond the Workplace

Leadership relationships are not confined to the walls of your organization. Engaging with your community, industry peers, and mentors expands your perspective and strengthens your leadership capabilities.

- **Community Engagement**: Participate in initiatives that align with your organization's values. This demonstrates your commitment to making a positive impact and builds relationships with stakeholders beyond your immediate team.

- **Mentorship**: Seek out mentors who can provide guidance and perspective, while also offering mentorship to emerging leaders. These relationships create a cycle of learning and growth.
- **Network with Intention**: Build connections with peers in your industry by attending conferences, joining professional groups, or participating in collaborative projects. Networking is not just about gaining contacts—it is about forming meaningful relationships that can inspire and challenge you.

Cultivating Psychological Safety

Psychological safety is the belief that team members can express themselves without fear of embarrassment, rejection, or punishment. It is a critical component of strong leadership relationships. When people feel safe, they are more likely to share ideas, take risks, and engage in meaningful dialogue.

As a leader, you can cultivate psychological safety by:

- Encourage open communication and feedback.
- Responding constructively to mistakes or failures.
- Demonstrating empathy and respect in every interaction.

A team that feels psychologically safe is not only more cohesive but also more innovative and resilient.

Leading with Servanthood

One of the most profound ways to build stronger relationships in leadership is to adopt a servant-leadership mindset. Servant leaders prioritize the needs of their team above their own, fostering a culture of mutual respect and collaboration. Servant leaders:

- **Empower Others**: Identify and nurture the strengths of your team members. Provide the resources, support, and opportunities they need to succeed.
- **Lead by Example**: Demonstrate the values and behaviors you want to see in your team. Your actions set the standard for the relationships you want to build.
- **Show Appreciation**: Regularly acknowledge the contributions of your team. Genuine gratitude strengthens bonds and motivates individuals to excel.

Leadership is not a solo endeavor. It is a collaborative effort built on the foundation of meaningful, supportive, and inspiring relationships.

In addition to building stronger relationships in leadership, you need to understand that leadership is both an art and a science. It requires a blend of emotional intelligence, relational intelligence, and practical strategies to create connections that are authentic, impactful, and enduring.

Chapter 9

Creating a Culture of Wellness at Work

In today's rapidly developing and high-stress world, fostering a culture of wellness has become more crucial than ever. A wellness culture at work is an organizational environment that actively promotes and supports the health and well-being of its employees. This culture encourages healthy habits, provides resources for physical and mental health, fosters a supportive and inclusive workplace, and prioritizes work-life balance.

As a leader, prioritizing the well-being of your employees and community members is key to creating a healthy, productive environment. Establishing a wellness culture yields numerous benefits, including enhanced employee satisfaction, reduced absenteeism, improved productivity, greater team cohesion, and lower healthcare costs. When employees are happy and healthy, they are more likely to be engaged, loyal, and motivated.

To cultivate a culture of wellness at work, you need to:

1. Lead by Example

One of the first steps in creating a culture of wellness is to lead by example. Your behavior sets the tone for your team and community. By prioritizing your own well-being and demonstrating healthy habits—such as taking regular breaks, practicing relaxation, exercising regularly, and maintaining a balanced diet—you can inspire others to do the same. Showing that you value your health encourages others to follow suit.

2. **Providing Resources and Support**

In addition to leading by example, it is crucial to offer resources and support for wellness initiatives in both the workplace and the community. This may include:

Health and Wellness Programs: Organize fitness challenges and workshops that promote well-being.

Healthy Office Options: Provide healthy office options and encourage nutritious eating habits.

Work-Life Balance: Promote policies that support a healthy balance between work and personal life, by creating a supportive environment. This results in you empowering employees and community members to prioritize their health and well-being.

3. **Foster Open Communications**

Furthermore, as a leader, fostering a culture of open communication and support is vital. Encourage employees and community members to share their wellness goals and challenges. Leaders could provide them with the resources they need to succeed. This could involve offering counseling services, hosting wellness workshops, or providing access to fitness facilities. A safe and supportive environment allows individuals to feel empowered to prioritize their health.

4. Assess Needs and Interests

This can be done by conducting employee surveys. Conduct comprehensive surveys to gauge the current health status, interests, and needs of employees. This information will help to design relevant and engaging programs.

You can also offer voluntary health risk assessments to identify common health issues within the team, such as stress levels, physical activity, and nutrition habits. Use aggregated data to tailor wellness initiatives.

5. Develop a Comprehensive Wellness Program

Your wellness program should include physical health, emotional health, and financial well-being.

Physical Health

Fitness Initiatives: Provide gym memberships, on-site fitness classes, or virtual workout sessions. Encourage participation by organizing group activities like walking meetings or fitness challenges.

Healthy Eating: Supply healthy snacks in the office, organize nutrition workshops, and partner with local businesses to offer discounts on healthy meals. Promote hydration by ensuring easy access to water.

Preventive Care: Offer flu shots, health screenings, and access to wellness coaches. Encourage regular medical check-ups and raise awareness about preventive health measures.

Mental and Emotional Health

Stress Management: Implement stress-relief programs, such as yoga, meditation, and relaxation workshops. Provide access to psychological counseling and support services.

Mental Health Training: Educate managers and employees about mental health and help them recognize signs of stress or burnout. This then reduces the stigma surrounding mental health. Equip them with tools to support themselves and their colleagues.

Flexible Work Options: Introduce flexible working hours, remote working policies, and job-sharing options to help employees effectively manage their personal and professional responsibilities.

Financial Well-being

Financial Education: Offer workshops on budgeting, saving, retirement planning, and debt management, in addition to, providing access to financial advisors.

Incentives and Benefits: Review your benefits package to ensure it includes financial wellness options such as retirement plans, health savings accounts (HSAs), and tuition reimbursement.

6. Create a supportive environment

Organize regular team-building events, social outings, and volunteer opportunities to foster camaraderie and strengthen relationships. Furthermore, promote an inclusive work environment where all employees feel respected and valued. Supporting employee resource groups and diversity initiatives helps to foster a healthy environment.

7. Recognition and Rewards

Celebrate Success: Recognize and reward employees for their contributions and achievements. Use both formal recognition programs and informal appreciation methods to maintain balance.

Evolving the Wellness Culture

Establishing a wellness culture at work is an evolving process that requires thoughtful consideration, strategic planning, and continuous effort. The goal is to foster an environment where employees feel valued, supported, and motivated to prioritize their health and well-being. This multifaceted approach encompasses physical, mental, and emotional health, while promoting positive social interactions and work-life balance.

Chapter 10

Time Management and Work-Life

Today's technology-driven world presents a unique set of challenges for leaders. Leaders often juggle numerous responsibilities, from strategic decision-making and team management to personal commitments and self-care. Achieving a harmonious balance between professional and personal life while effectively managing time is essential for sustainable success. This chapter explores the fundamentals of time management and maintaining a healthy work-life balance, while offering strategies and actionable steps to help leaders thrive both professionally and personally.

The Essence of Time Management

Time is the most finite resource leaders have. Unlike money or materials, once time is spent, it can never be reclaimed. Recognizing its value is the first step towards effective time management.

The Pareto Principle (80/20 Rule)

This principle suggests that 80% of outcomes come from 20% of efforts. Leaders must identify and focus on the tasks that yield the highest impact on their goals. Prioritizing high-value activities ensures optimal use of time.

The Eisenhower Matrix

The Eisenhower Matrix helps leaders prioritize tasks based on their urgency and importance. It divides tasks into four quadrants:

- Urgent and Important
- Important but Not Urgent
- Urgent but Not Important
- Not Urgent and Not Important

By focusing primarily on tasks that are important but not urgent, leaders can work proactively rather than reactively.

Strategies for Effective Time Management

1. Set Clear Goals and Priorities

Famed author Stephen Covey once said, "The key is not to prioritize what's on your schedule, but to schedule your priorities." A crucial aspect of effective time management is the ability to discern what demands your attention and what can wait. Start each day by identifying key tasks that align with both your professional goals and personal values.

2. Delegate Effectively

Leadership is not about doing everything yourself; it is about harnessing the strengths of those around you. Delegate tasks that others can handle, allowing you to focus on high-impact activities that require your expertise. This not only empowers your team but also alleviates unnecessary stress on your shoulders.

3. **Utilize Technology**

Technology can be a powerful ally in time management. Tools like project management software, calendars, and communication platforms streamline workflows and enhance productivity.

4. **Practice the Two-Minute Rule**

If a task takes less than two minutes to complete, do it immediately. This prevents small tasks from piling up and becoming overwhelming.

5. **Time Blocking**

Segmenting your day into distinct blocks dedicated to specific tasks can greatly enhance focus and productivity. Allocate time for deep work, meetings, administrative tasks, and personal activities. This structured approach minimizes distractions and ensures that each aspect of your role receives due attention.

6. **Set Boundaries**

Healthy leaders establish clear boundaries between work and personal life. Defining work hours, limiting after-hours communication, and setting aside personal time are essential steps toward achieving balance.

7. Prioritize Self-Care

You must prioritize your well-being by incorporating activities that promote physical, mental, and emotional health. Regular exercise, proper nutrition, adequate sleep, and relaxation practices are crucial components of self-care.

8. Embrace Flexibility

Rigid schedules can lead to burnout. Embracing flexibility allows you to adapt to unexpected changes while maintaining productivity. This could involve flexible work hours or the ability to work remotely.

9. Quality Time with Loved Ones

Investing quality time with family and friends nurture relationships and provides a support system. You should schedule regular family time and social activities to foster a sense of connection and fulfillment.

10. Daily Reflection

Spend a few minutes at the end of each day reflecting on your achievements, areas for improvement, and how well you adhered to your priorities. This reflection fosters a growth mindset and helps you realign your focus.

11. Plan Ahead

Sunday evenings or early Monday mornings are perfect times to plan your week. Outline your primary goals, schedule crucial meetings, and allocate time for personal activities. Having a clear roadmap for the week reduces anxiety and boosts productivity.

12. Seek Support Systems

Engage with peer groups, coaching networks, or support forums. Sharing experiences and challenges with fellow leaders provides fresh perspectives, solutions, and reassurance that you are not alone in your journey.

13. Practice Gratitude

Keep a gratitude journal. Regularly noting down things you are thankful for fosters a positive mindset and mitigates the adverse effects of stress. Gratitude reaffirms what is going well and highlights the positive aspects of life and work.

Chapter 11

Sustaining Wellness for Long Term Leadership Success

Leadership success is not achieved overnight; it requires dedication, hard work, and continuous learning. Successful leaders are those who inspire, motivate, and empower others to reach their full potential. In this chapter, we will explore the key principles and strategies that can help you on the path to leadership success.

The Qualities of a Successful Leader

- ✓ **Vision:** Successful leaders have a clear vision of where they want to go and are able to articulate this vision to others. They inspire their team members to work towards a common goal and create a sense of purpose and direction.

- ✓ **Communication:** Effective communication is essential for leadership success. Leaders must be able to listen actively, provide feedback, and communicate clearly and concisely to ensure their message is understood by all team members.

- ✓ **Emotional Intelligence:** Successful leaders possess high emotional intelligence, which allows them to understand and manage their own emotions and those of others. They are empathetic, self-aware, and able to build strong relationships with their team members.

✓ **Adaptability:** In today's fast-paced and ever-changing business environment, successful leaders must be adaptable and flexible. They are able to navigate uncertainty, embrace change, and pivot when necessary to achieve their goals.

✓ **Decision-Making:** Leaders are often faced with tough decisions and the ability to make sound, timely decisions is crucial for success. Successful leaders gather information, weigh the pros and cons, and make decisions based on data and intuition.

Strategies for Leadership Success

Set Clear Goals: Define your long-term and short-term goals and create a roadmap for how you plan to achieve them. Break down your goals into actionable steps and track your progress regularly.

Develop Your Skills: Continuous learning and development are important to leadership success. Invest in training, workshops, and coaching to enhance your skills, as well as staying current with industry trends.

Build a Strong Team: Surround yourself with talented individuals who complement your strengths and weaknesses. Delegate tasks, empower your team members, and provide opportunities for growth and development.

Lead by Example: Demonstrate the qualities and behaviors you expect from your team members. Be ethical, trustworthy, consistent in your actions, and inspire others through your words and deeds.

Embrace Feedback: Seek feedback from your team members, peers, and mentors to identify areas for improvement and growth. Use feedback as an opportunity to learn and evolve as a leader.

Foster a Positive Culture: Create a positive work environment where team members feel valued, respected, and motivated to do their best work. Celebrate successes, address conflicts promptly, and promote open communication.

Leadership success is a journey that requires commitment, self-awareness, and a willingness to learn and grow. By embodying the qualities of a successful leader, setting clear goals, developing your skills, and fostering a positive culture. By doing these, you can pave the way for your own success and the success of your team. Remember, leadership is not about titles or positions; it is about making a positive impact, inspiring others, and achieving collective goals. Embrace the challenges, seize the opportunities, and lead with purpose and passion on your path to leadership success.

Chapter 12

Essential Lifestyle Changes for Optimal Well-Being

In our pursuit of a healthier, more fulfilling life, small yet impactful lifestyle adjustments can lead to profound transformation. Here are twelve essential changes to consider as you embark on your journey toward well-being:

1. Prioritize Whole Foods:

Replace processed foods with a vibrant array of fruits and vegetables to nourish your body. Prioritizing these whole foods can enhance your overall health.

2. Hydrate Wisely:

Exchange sodas and sugary beverages for refreshing water infused with lemon which will promote hydration and vitality without the added sugars.

3. Incorporate Nutrient-Dense Foods:

Increase your intake of nuts and whole grains, which provide essential nutrients and sustain your energy levels throughout the day.

4. Establish a Restful Sleep Routine:

Aim for 7-9 hours of restorative sleep each night. Prioritize going to bed early to allow your body to rejuvenate and recover fully.

5. Embrace Daily Movement:

Commit to walking for 20-30 minutes each day. This simple yet effective practice supports cardiovascular health and boosts your mood.

6. Cultivate Meaningful Connections:

Spend quality time with loved ones and prioritize laughter. Strengthening these relationships enhances emotional well-being and fosters a sense of belonging.

7. Engage in Spiritual Growth:

Dedicate time to reading the Bible and practicing positive affirmations. These activities can deepen your spiritual connection and promote a positive mindset.

8. Practice Deep breathing and Meditation:

Incorporate these practices into your daily routine to reduce stress, improve focus, and enhance emotional well-being.

9. Limit Screen Time:

Be mindful of your screen time, especially before bed. Reducing exposure to screens can improve sleep quality and overall mental health.

10. Stay Active Mentally:

Engage in activities that challenge your brain, such as puzzles, learning new skills, or taking up a new hobby. This can help maintain cognitive health as you age.

11. Establish a Gratitude Practice:

Take a few moments each day to reflect on what you're grateful for. This practice can shift your mindset to a more positive outlook on life.

12. Prioritize Self-Care:

Make time for self-care activities that rejuvenate you, whether it's taking a relaxing bath, enjoying a hobby, or spending time in nature.

CONCLUSION

In a world that is increasingly complex and demanding, the role of a leader extends far beyond the confines of traditional management. Effective leadership requires a comprehensive approach that encompasses mental, physical, and spiritual well-being. As we have explored throughout this book, these three dimensions are intricately interconnected, each influencing the other. Together, they can shape a leader's ability to inspire, motivate, and guide their teams.

Mental well-being is the foundation upon which effective leadership is built. A clear, focused mind enables leaders to make informed decisions, tackle challenges with resilience, and cultivate a culture of innovation. When leaders prioritize their mental health, they demonstrate the importance of emotional intelligence, fostering trust and open communication within their teams.

Physical well-being is equally crucial. A healthy body fuels energy, stamina, and productivity. Leaders who invest in their physical health set an example for their teams, encouraging a culture of wellness that enhances overall performance and morale. By recognizing the importance of physical fitness, leaders can better manage stress, avoid burnout, and maintain the vitality needed to lead with confidence.

Spiritual well-being, often overlooked in the corporate world, brings a profound sense of purpose and connection. Leaders who cultivate their spiritual health—whether through mindfulness, reflection, or a commitment to their values—are better equipped to navigate ethical dilemmas, inspire loyalty, and create a shared vision that resonates with their teams. This dimension of well-being fosters a sense of belonging and community, essential for building cohesive and resilient organizations.

Ultimately, a leader's effectiveness is deeply rooted in their ability to integrate these three facets of well-being. When leaders prioritize their mental, physical, and spiritual health, they not only enhance their own performance but also empower those around them to thrive.

As you move forward in your leadership journey, remember that your well-being is not a luxury; it is a necessity. By committing to your own holistic health, you are not only investing in your success but also in the success of your team and organization. Embrace this journey with intention, and inspire others to do the same. Together, we can cultivate a new era of leadership—one that is grounded in well-being, authenticity, and a shared commitment to making a positive impact in the world.

ABOUT THE AUTHOR

Eva M. Francis

HC, MSN, CCRN, NEA-BC

Inspirational, Visionary, Compassionate, Adaptable, Collaborative and Accountable: These are just some of the traits that describe Eva M. Francis. A former accomplished healthcare and hospital executive, she has successfully transformed organizational cultures, leading to improved hospital and departmental efficiency, multiple accreditations, leadership development, and overall enhanced healthcare services.

Eva M. Francis is a results-oriented leader with a proven track record of driving organizations toward optimized business processes, effective clinical operations, superior patient care services, and improved quality measures, all while enhancing hospital operations and increasing bottom-line results.

A transformational leader and strategic clinical program developer, Eva brings extensive experience working on high-profile leadership and healthcare projects. Her expertise spans business development, restructuring, expansion, and strategic planning. She inspires leaders and staff by fostering performance-based cultures, instituting coaching and mentoring programs, and emphasizing collaboration, often partnering with leaders across various industries.

Eva began her career as a registered nurse in her native, Jamaica, before migrating to the U.S., where she completed both her undergraduate and graduate degrees at Florida Atlantic University. Through her dedication and passion for nursing, she quickly ascended to the role of nurse executive, becoming a respected and trusted voice in her field.

She has inspired, mentored, and trained thousands of healthcare professionals and leaders. An award-winning leader, author, professional speaker, and certified leadership teacher and trainer with the John Maxwell Team, Eva is a highly motivated individual, deeply involved in community projects. She firmly believes that everyone is born with a unique gift meant to add value to others' lives and lives by the principle, "To whom much is given, much is required."

Eva M. Francis, HC, RN, MSN, CCRN,

Author

Motivational Speaker

Executive Leadership

Healthcare Business Consultant

www.ingramcontent.com/pod-product-compliance
Lightning Source LLC
Chambersburg PA
CBHW070213230526
45471CB00002B/937